I0164084

How Can We Walk

in Forgiveness?

Doug Roberts

How Can We Walk in Forgiveness?

by Doug Roberts

Copyright © 2019 Doug Roberts

Published by:
Doug Roberts Publishing
P. O. Box 321
Frederick, Oklahoma 73542

All rights reserved. No part of this book may be reproduced or transmitted in any form or by any means (electronic or mechanical, including photocopying, recording, or by any information storage and retrieval system) without written permission from the author, except for brief quotations in book reviews.

All Scriptures have been taken from the New American Standard Bible® (NASB), Copyright © 1960, 1962, 1963, 1968, 1971, 1972, 1973, 1975, 1977, 1995 by The Lockman Foundation. Used by permission. www.Lockman.org

ISBN: 978-0-9825992-2-9-7

I want to say thank you to Ed Chinn, Fred White, Rob Hatch, Shellie Kushnerick and Rita Roberts for all their help in getting this into print.

Printed in the United States of America

Table of Contents

Chapter 1 The High Cost of Unforgiveness

I'm going to tell you about one of the keys that is crucial to walking in the fullness of what the Father has for us on the earth.

That key is learning how to walk in forgiveness.

Unforgiveness is certainly one of the largest tools in the devil's toolbox. And, he uses it to keep many of us from walking in the Father's kingdom. I'm going to share some Scriptures that will, first, reveal the importance of forgiving. Second, they will show you how to walk in forgiveness.

I want to start in Matthew 18:24-35. It's a familiar parable, about the king settling an account with a slave that owed him money.

"And when he had begun to settle them, there was brought to him one who owed him ten thousand talents. But since he did not have the means to repay, his lord commanded him to be sold, along with his wife and children and all that he had, and repayment to be made. The slave therefore falling down, prostrated himself before him, saying, 'Have patience with me, and I will repay you everything.' And the lord of that slave felt compassion and released him and forgave him the debt." Matthew 18: 24-27 NASB

Do we understand, the slave owed the King more money than he could *ever* pay? Some scholars estimate he owed the US dollar equivalent of $160 million! But, whatever the amount, it was more than he could pay in several lifetimes. But the king felt compassion and forgave him his debt. All of it.

Let's think about the Father's love for us. Because of our sins, there was no way we could repay on our own. We could *never* come into the fullness of the Father's purpose for us. We could simply never earn the gift of God. But, God in His mercy, God in His love, gave us Jesus. And Jesus paid the price for our sin. And, God forgave us all of our debt against us, because of the blood of Jesus Christ.

So, how did the slave respond? The king had just forgiven the slave all—millions!—that was owed to him. But when the slave left the king's presence, debt free…

"…that slave went out and found one of his fellow slaves who owed him a hundred denarii; and he seized him and began to choke him, saying, 'Pay back what you owe.' So, his fellow slave fell down and began to entreat him, saying, 'Have patience with me and I will repay you.'" Matthew 18:28 NASB

Incredibly, the king had just forgiven that man a debt he couldn't pay. But then that same man found a fellow servant that owed him a small amount. And the man begged, "Have patience, I'll repay."

And the Bible tells us the rest of the story:

"He was unwilling however, but went and threw him in prison until he should pay back what was owed. So when his fellow slaves saw what had happened, they were deeply grieved and came and reported to their lord all that had happened. Then summoning him, his lord said to him, 'You wicked slave, I forgave you all that debt because you entreated me. Should you not also have had mercy on your fellow slave, even as I had mercy on you?' And his lord, moved with anger, handed him over to the torturers until he should repay all that was owed him." Matthew 18:30-34 NASB

What a story of a shocking lack of patience and compassion. But, now look at the very next verse, the real point of this story:

"So shall My heavenly Father also do to you, if each of you does not forgive his brother from your heart." Matthew 18:35

That verse, that amazing statement, should stop us all cold in our tracks. It says that the way the Lord has shown us mercy is the standard by which we are to have mercy on others! Think of it; the way the Lord forgave us is the very way we are to forgive others. And, if we don't forgive as He does, He will not forgive us!

if we don't forgive as He does, He will not forgive us.

That is a truly frightening thing.

And, let me also tell you that I have read the Scripture for many years, and this passage is the only place I have found that provides for a forgiven debt to be reinstated. Unforgiveness can wipe out a forgiven debt. Because this servant did not forgive, then the debt that he owed was fully restored to the full amount owed.

And it also tells us that our heavenly Father will do the same to us."

Now, I know that some may say, "That doesn't seem fair." Well, God is a righteous God; He is a just God. But, His fairness doesn't fit into the way we humans categorize fairness. That is why it's so essential for us to learn how to walk in forgiveness, mercy, grace and all the things God has for us.

Unforgiveness will not rob you of your eternal salvation; that price has already been paid for by Jesus Christ. But, that's not the point. Unforgiveness *will* prevent us from walking on the earth in the full provision of the things God has for us here.

And that is a very high cost.

Chapter 2 Forgive Us as We Forgive Others

Let's look further into the Word of the Lord about the importance of walking in forgiveness. The Word tells us:

"And whenever you stand praying, forgive, if you have anything against anyone; so that your Father also who is in heaven may forgive you your transgressions." Mark 11:25 NASB

The first thing we're told to do when we stand to pray is to allow the Holy Spirit to search our heart to see if we hold any unforgiveness toward anyone. That scripture uses two significant words: "Anything" and "anyone." That covers everything and everybody. In other words, there's not anything or anyone that we can hold, and not forgive, according to the Scriptures.

The very next verse says:

"But if you do not forgive, neither will your Father who is in heaven forgive your transgressions." Mark 11:26 NASB

So, we've now read two references, from different gospels, where it talks about our Father forgiving us in accordance with how we forgive others. Let's look at how Jesus taught us to pray.

"Pray, then, in this way:
    'Our Father who art in heaven,
    Hallowed be Thy name.
    'Thy kingdom come.
    Thy will be done,
    On earth as it is in heaven.
'Give us this day our daily bread.
'And forgive us our debts, as we also have forgiven our debtors.
'And do not lead us into temptation, but deliver us from evil.

For Thine is the kingdom, and the power, and the glory, forever. Amen." Matthew 6: 9-13 NASB

Did you catch that? Jesus' model prayer includes "And forgive us our debts as we have forgiven our debtors."

We may not like that. But, when Jesus taught His disciples (and all of us) how to pray, He said, "Pray this way: Father, forgive me, just like I have forgiven my debtors." Forgive me…just like I have forgiven my brothers and sisters in Christ. Forgive me…just like I have forgiven my family. Forgive me…just like I have forgiven the people in my office. Forgive me…just like I forgive the other drivers around me in rush hour.

Do we really want God to forgive us the way we have forgiven others?

Do we really want God to forgive us the way we have forgiven others? Think about that. Do we want Him to forgive us our debts "just as" we have forgiven our debt?

9

And then, as if He wants to make sure we got it in the prayer, Jesus goes on in verse 14 and 15, the first verses *after* the prayer:

"For if you forgive men for their transgressions, your heavenly Father will also forgive you. But if you do not forgive men, then your Father will not forgive your transgressions." Matthew 6:14-15 NASB

God said He has predestined us for good works in Christ, so we need to have an understanding of the importance of forgiveness. If we walk in unforgiveness, that can hinder us in the things God has called us to do.

Let's look further into how to walk in forgiveness. John's gospel says:

"If you forgive the sins of any, their sins have been forgiven them; if you retain the sins of any, they have been retained." John 20:23 NASB

When we forgive, the sins are forgiven, they're done away with. But if we don't forgive, those sins are retained. Where have they been retained? I believe they're retained in my heart.

For example, if someone offended you and you haven't forgiven them, the next time you see that person, what's the first thing that comes to your mind? You remember what they did to you. If that's what's in you—if you hold it in your heart— obviously you hold onto unforgiveness. You have *retained* the offense.

To not forgive one who offended you is like you drinking poison, hoping the offender will die. Unforgiveness kills *you*, it doesn't hurt the person that you have not forgiven.

That is why we continually need to ask the Holy Spirit to search our heart, to see if we have any unforgiveness toward anyone.

Now, to help you see how this works in the Church, let's consider Paul's word to Ephesians.

Therefore, laying aside falsehood, SPEAK TRUTH, EACH ONE of you, WITH HIS NEIGHBOR, for we are members of one another. BE ANGRY, AND yet DO NOT SIN; do not let the sun go down on your anger, and do not give the devil an opportunity. Let him who steals steal no longer; but rather let him labor, performing with his own hands what is good, in order that he may have something to share with him who has need. Let no unwholesome word proceed from your mouth, but only such a word as is good for edification according to the need of the moment, that it may give grace to those who hear. And do not grieve the Holy Spirit of God, by whom you were sealed for the day of redemption. Let all bitterness and wrath and anger and clamor and slander be put away from you, along with all malice. Ephesians 4:25-31 NASB

Sometimes we all fail to walk in forgiveness, speak the truth, or speak wholesome words. Or, we get angry or speak out of bitterness. But, when we fall into that trap of sin, we're doing two things; we're giving an opportunity to the devil, and we're grieving the Holy Spirit.

Look, I believe in the power of the blood of Christ. I believe that all authority has been given to me in Jesus' name. But, I also believe that when I give the devil an opportunity, he's going to take advantage of that opportunity and come in and rule and reign and be lord in my life in that area — in the area of my disobedience.

Sometimes, we wonder why nothing happens when we pray. Or, we may wonder why we're going through difficult situations. It may come down to this: who is the lord in that area of your life right now? If I come to your town and you give me the key to your house, and I unlock the door and come in, am I an intruder? No, you invited me in and gave me the key to your home. But, if I come to your town and I break the window to get into your house, what happens? I'm an intruder because I don't have the key. I don't have permission to get into your home.

If I have your permission to enter your house and do so, you can't file charges against me. But, if I *don't* have permission, you can file charges against me for trespassing. It is the same way in the spiritual world. If Satan enters our house, we can file charges and evict him. But, if we gave him the key, we invited the problem. And that's going to take longer to get rid of him.

Unforgiveness is a key that we sometimes give the devil. In so doing, we give him the opportunity to rob us of the authority and blessings of the Lord.

I think unforgiveness is a key that we sometimes give the devil. In so doing, we provide him the opportunity to rob us of the authority and blessings of the Lord. Paul is telling us not to let that happen. We need to be "Forgiving each other, just as God, in Christ, also forgave you."

In the next chapter, I want to continue to examine the power of keys in our walk with the Lord.

Chapter 3   Who Holds the
Keys to Your Life?

How did God forgive us in Christ? God forgave us with the gift of Jesus Christ. God gave the best he had for our sin. So when God sees us, he doesn't see us in our sin, he sees us in the gift that he gave us in Jesus Christ. That's why Paul wrote, "I have been crucified with Christ; and it is no longer I who live, but Christ lives in me; and the *life* which I now live in the flesh I live by faith in the Son of God, who loved me, and delivered Himself up for me." (Galatians 2:20, NASB)

Anything "in Christ" is amazing. The best I can do outside of Christ is death. The worst I can do in Christ is amazing.

God sees us in Christ. And anything "in Christ" is amazing. Anything outside of Christ is sin. The best I can do outside of Christ is death. The worst I can do in

Christ is amazing.

I believe that so many of us miss out on what God has for us because we have chosen to give the devil a key to our house. And we offer that key to him by not walking in forgiveness, by not walking in the gifts of the Spirit, by not guarding our heart.

Do you realize that you bless yourself or curse yourself by what comes out of your mouth? Blessing and cursing are keys. Who has the key? You do. So, who did you give it to? Who is the lord of your life today? If you gave a key to the devil, you gave him an opportunity to rule and reign in your life again. You invited him back in. No, it's not permanent. And, yes, you can order him off the property. But, this is serious business. That's why we need to allow the Holy Spirit to examine in our lives.

I want to consider this Scripture, which holds a powerful key.

"But whom you forgive anything, I forgive also; for indeed what I have forgiven, if I have forgiven anything, I did it for your sakes in the presence of

Christ, in order that no advantage be taken of us by Satan; for we are not ignorant of his schemes." 2 Corinthians 2: 10-11 NASB

In that passage, Paul says that whoever you forgive for anything, I forgive also. I think we have another key here of not taking up other people's offenses. For an example, your friend "Bob" was offended by "George," and, even though George didn't do anything to you, you took up Bob's offense against George?

But then, the Holy Spirit started dealing with Bob and telling him, "Hey, you're carrying some unforgiveness in your heart toward George." So Bob asked George to forgive him. But, when you saw Bob and George golfing together, you thought (and maybe said) "How can Bob have fellowship with that guy? Doesn't he remember what George did?" Now you have judged both—Bob and George—and that judgment against them gave the devil a key to your house! And he will use it to rob you of your fellowship with both brothers. So, taking up someone else's offense is just as bad as being the one offended, maybe even worse.

How many times have we been quick to take up someone else's offense when the "offender" did nothing to us. We just came alongside a friend, and before we realize what happened, we took up someone else's offense. When we do that, the devil comes in and takes advantage of the judgments that we made. He takes advantage of our unforgiveness that we've held. All because we joined with someone else's offense.

It's not our place to take up someone else's offense. It's our place to bless and curse not. It's our place to intercede and pray for reconciliation. The Scripture says in 2 Corinthians 5:18 we've all been given the ministry of reconciliation. So if you see your brother, "Bob," hurting from the relational breach with George, and you have a relationship with Bob and George, your job is to reconcile and be a peacemaker, not to take up the offense and be the   judge.

Chapter 4   How to Walk as "Chosen by God"

"And so, as those who have been chosen of God, holy and beloved, put on a heart of compassion, kindness, humility, gentleness and patience; bearing with one another, and forgiving each other, whoever has a complaint against anyone; just as the Lord forgave you, so also should you. And beyond all these things put on love, which is the perfect bond of unity. And let the peace of Christ rule in your hearts, to which indeed you were called in one body; and be thankful. Let the word of Christ richly dwell within you, with all wisdom teaching and admonishing one another with psalms and hymns and spiritual songs, singing with thankfulness in your hearts to God.

And whatever you do in word or deed, do all in the name of the Lord Jesus, giving thanks through Him to God the Father." Colossians 3:12-17 NASB

Have you been chosen of God? In this passage above, Paul says, "Yes, you have been chosen of God." So, this must be speaking to you and me. So, if we're the ones God is talking to, what is He saying that we should do?

We are to "put on" these things like we would put on a coat. Specifically, we are to walk in a heart of compassion. And, kindness, humility, gentleness, and patience. We are to bear with one another, and we are to forgive whoever has a complaint against anyone.

That covers everything. There's not any weakness or sin in anyone that we can't forgive and bless and then walk together in reconciliation.

Our big job is to guard our heart. I can't help what's in someone else's heart, but I can guard my heart. So I ask the Lord to examine my heart. Holy Spirit, come search my ways, reveal anything in my heart that's displeasing to you so I can deal with it. I don't want to be robbed of God's provision because of my ignorance and because of the things I've done to allow the enemy to come in and rule my life.

Let's look at what Jesus told His disciples:

"But I say to you who hear, love your enemies, do good to those who hate you, bless those who curse you, pray for those who mistreat you. Whoever hits you on the cheek, offer him the other also; and whoever takes away your coat, do not withhold your shirt from him either. Give to everyone who asks of you, and whoever takes away what is yours, do not demand it back. And just as you want people to treat you, treat them in the same way. And if you love those who love you, what credit is that to you? For even sinners love those who love them. And if you do good to those who do good to you, what credit is that to you?

For even sinners do the same. And if you lend to those from whom you expect to receive, what credit is that to you? Even sinners lend to sinners, in order to receive back the same amount. But love your enemies, and do good, and lend, expecting nothing in return; and your reward will be great, and you will be sons of the Most High; for He Himself is kind to ungrateful and evil men. Be merciful, just as your Father is merciful. And do not judge and you will not be judged; and do not condemn, and you will not be condemned; pardon, and you will be pardoned." Luke 6:27-37 NASB

If Jesus, the Son, said this to His disciples, do you think it may be essential for us too? We may not like these Scriptures, but we have to live in them. We don't get to choose His words; we only get to decide whether we obey or not.

Jesus said, "Love your enemies, do good to those who hate you." You can't do that all by yourself, in the strength of your own flesh. The only way we can do these things is to walk in the Spirit. In other words, we have to walk in the revelation that the Holy Spirit gives us. We must walk as sons and daughters of God.

We can't please God in our flesh. Part of the Christian walk is learning how to walk as Jesus walked on the earth. We must walk as He did, "because as He is, so also are we in this world." (1 John 4:17).

There's more. He said, "Love your enemies. Do good to those who hate you. Bless those who curse you." Walking in these kingdom principles will open up the provision of what God has for you.

God wants to see you prosper on the earth. He desires for you to walk in the fulfillment of what He has for you. And to help us, He's given us everything we need. He's given us faith, He's given us Jesus, He's given us the Holy Spirit.

So, it's not God's fault that we're not walking in what He said to do. If we're not walking in the

If we're not walking in the
fullness of what He said to do,
it's because we've chosen not to

fullness of what He said to do, it's because we've chosen not to put the Word into application in our life. And, by that failure, we have offered the devil access. We've given the devil position in our life. And the devil is the one that comes to rob, steal, and destroy. These are some of the foundational truths on how his chosen ones are to walk into full blessing of what the Father has for us.

Finally, let's look at the words of Peter.

"To sum up, all of you be harmonious, sympathetic, brotherly, kindhearted, and humble in spirit, not returning evil for evil or insult for insult, but giving a blessing instead. For you were called for this very purpose that you might inherit a blessing. The one who desires life, to love and see good days, must keep his tongue from evil and his lips from speaking deceit. He must turn away from evil and do good. He must seek peace and pursue it. For the eyes of the Lord are toward the righteous and his ear attends to their prayer, But the face of the Lord is against those who do evil." 1 Peter 3:8-12 NASB

Here, Peter tells us more of how to walk as God's chosen ones. And, then he basically tells us that if we do that, the eyes of the Lord will look face-to-face, eyeball-to-eyeball with us. But if we don't His face His will be against us.

When we're walking in what God calls us to do, then the eyes of the Lord are looking at us, his ears are open to us. Why? 1 Chronicles 16:9 explains, "For the eyes of the LORD move to and fro throughout the earth that He may strongly support those whose heart is completely His."

Do you want Him to give you strong support? If so, walk as those He has chosen. And that means to live in His Kingdom. I'll explain that in the next chapter.

Chapter 5 How To Live in the Kingdom

So, what have we learned so far?

When we walk in unforgiveness, we grieve the Holy Spirit, and we give the devil an opportunity. Those are severe consequences of not walking as His chosen ones. I don't want any of those. But, we can walk in the blessing of the Lord. We can please the Holy Spirit. We don't have to give the devil an opportunity; we can behold the goodness of the Lord. I want to see the face of the Lord. I want his ears to be open to my prayers.

The best way to find that place in the Lord is to embrace and walk in His Kingdom. Here is how Paul described that walk.

"Bless those who persecute you; bless and curse not. Rejoice with those who rejoice, and weep with those who weep. Be of the same mind toward one another; do not be haughty in mind, but associate with the lowly. Do not be wise in your own estimation. Never pay back evil for evil to anyone. Respect what is right in the sight of all men. If possible, so far as it depends on you, be at peace with all men. Never take your own revenge, beloved, but leave room for the wrath of God, for it is written, 'VENGEANCE IS MINE, I WILL REPAY,' says the Lord. 'BUT IF YOUR ENEMY IS HUNGRY, FEED HIM, AND IF HE IS THIRSTY, GIVE HIM A DRINK; FOR IN SO DOING YOU WILL HEAP BURNING COALS UPON HIS HEAD.' Do not be overcome by evil, but overcome evil with good." Romans 12:14-21 NASB

So many times, when we judge sinners in the world, we forget that they're just living up to their standards. They don't know the Lord. They're not baptized in the Holy Spirit. They don't have eternal life. So the only thing they know is the world and its culture.

But, if we are citizens of His Kingdom, then we are not of the world's culture, we are of the kingdom's culture. If we are in Christ, our minds are renewed and we become better citizens of His Kingdom. If we are in Christ, our vision becomes aligned with His vision. By knowing and understanding who we are in Christ, then the expression of who He is will be seen on the earth.

As His sons and daughters, His fatherhood in our lives will cause us to live by a new standard. The way we live, the way we maintain our love and the way we walk in forgiveness sets the standard that the world can see. At his final gathering with His disciples, Jesus told them, "By this all men will know that you are My disciples, if you have love for one another." (John 13:35)

So, by this, you can see why the devil wants us to walk in unforgiveness, why he wants us to return evil for evil, and why he wants us to curse and not bless.

Even the devil knows that when we start doing the things God called us to do in Christ, when we start loving one another, then the world is going to know that God sent his Son.

God has called us to rule and not react. If you believe that, then how do we rule? Well, here's an example. Ruling is when someone speaks evil to you, you bless them. When someone hits you, you turn your other cheek. When someone curses you, you do good to them. God has called us to rule in the earth. So let's be rulers and not reactors.

Remember the authority that has been given to those who believe.

I want to leave you with three simple, but life-changing, principles of walking in His Kingdom:

1.   When people curse you and hurt you, forgive them. And then, as Michael O'Shields has taught in his book, *Rethinking Forgiveness,* send them a blessing. In that way the next time you see them, you won't remember their offense to you. You will remember the blessing you gave to them. That's how God forgave us in Christ. We offended God, but He gave us the blessing of Jesus Christ. So now when God sees us, He doesn't see us as the offender we were; He sees us through the gift of the blessing that He gave us in Jesus Christ.

2.   Love one another the way you want to be loved. Forgive one another the way you want to be forgiven. Be careful what comes out of your mouth.

3.   Ask the Holy Spirit to show you if you have any unforgiveness or judgments in your heart towards anyone.

Now I want to lead you in a prayer.
Father, I see that I have made a judgment, and I have chosen not to forgive. So, right now, I choose to forgive, and I choose to release my judgments.

And I choose to bless those who have hurt me. And I choose to walk in forgiveness.

Father, I thank you for stopping the reaping of this unforgiveness and judgment in my life, in Jesus' name. Amen.

Ha Ha Ha on you devil, you are not going to steal my destiny.

Group Discussion Guide

In order to allow the message of this book to penetrate the soil of your mind and heart, Doug and those who stand close to him in these things have prepared this guide of questions and discussion issues to help you work these truths into your life.

Do you see that unforgiveness can be very expensive?

Do you want God to forgive you as you have forgiven others?

Doug wrote, "To not forgive one who offended you is like drinking poison, hoping the offender will die." Can you give an example of that?

How does failing to forgive provide an opportunity to the devil to enter into your life?

How does failing to forgive grieve the Holy Spirit?

Have you ever given a life-key to the devil? What happened?

Do you see the danger of taking up another person's offense?

What does "ministry of reconciliation" mean to you?

How can we walk as Jesus did upon the earth?

Do you want the eyes of the Lord upon you, as described in 2 Chronicles 16:9? Why?

How can we be citizens of the Kingdom of God *and*, at the same time, citizens of our nation, state, or city?

Doug wrote that we are to "rule and not react." What does that mean to you?

www.ingramcontent.com/pod-product-compliance
Lightning Source LLC
Chambersburg PA
CBHW020442030426
42337CB00014B/1360

* 9 7 8 0 9 8 2 5 9 9 2 9 7 *